25-Day JOURNAL

LEARN KEY SKILLS TO NAVIGATE YOUR LIFE, MAKE GOOD DECISIONS AND MANAGE YOUR WELL-BEING

BIANCA SAPARA-GRANT

First paperback edition March 2022
Version 1.0

www.parentpower-ed.co.uk

Leyton Village Publishing

ISBN: 978-1-7397122-0-4

This journal belongs to

....

IF FOUND, PLEASE CONTACT ME

Email ....

Social ....

Mobile ....

Contents

Introduction

Hello!

Thank you for opening this journal!

You're perhaps being told that you are living in the best time of your life. That you must access opportunities to grow, develop, explore and fulfil your potential as you transition from a young person into an adult. But it can be hard to see *how* this is true. On the flip side, you're also being told that you are too young to do a lot of things. So surely being older is better? Because right now, you don't have your own money and life feels tough. School. Teachers. Parents or Carers. Friends. Expectations. Not having all the stuff that you want. Not having the freedom you want. How can this possibly be the best time of your life?

What the grown-ups (maybe groan-ups?) in your life mean is that this is the best time to discover and build crucial knowledge, skills and strengths, so that when opportunities appear, or hard moments knock you over, you are ready. Your development is so much more than just your educational path. It's about being able to navigate the world and all the choices that you'll be faced with. It's about making good decisions and even creating your own opportunities. It's also about having a healthy relationship with yourself and others.

The 25-day journal will help you lay a solid foundation for your life and help you in your present and future. You will learn to observe and serve your mental health and well-being, make good decisions, develop good friendships, use your network for support and offer them support too. This is all important for your success and achievement (whatever success and achievement means to you).

The completion of the journal will provide you with the ability to:

- identify and acquire essential skills to support you in becoming your best;
- feel more prepared for your present and future;
- learn to rely on the support of the good people in your life;
- develop a sense of purpose, confidence, perseverance and resilience – all key to making you feel alive and proud;
- see your potential and use it;
- anticipate difficulties, handle setbacks and keep moving forward;
- see problems as solvable;
- see new experiences as opportunities to continuously learn and grow.

The 25-days represent 25 skills, habits and approaches to problems in life for you to **practise**. The key word is 'practise' because these things can be learnt, and practice (making the effort) is the only way to integrate these skills into your life. It is also important to acknowledge and tell yourself that there will be moments when you do well and other moments when you don't do well. That's OK. Don't expect hardcore skills that you can apply like learning to ride a bike or learning to swim. These are about growing and learning as a person and that won't cease until you choose to stop making an effort.

The 25 skills are broken down into sections as follows:

1. Recognise your strengths
2. Believe in yourself
3. Set yourself goals
4. Find your motivation
5. Handle anxiety
6. Be resourceful
7. Make smart choices
8. Prioritise your well-being
9. Be kind
10. Be a problem-solver
11. Have a growth mindset
12. Be curious
13. Increase positive self-talk
14. Cultural and civic skills
15. Use humour
16. Be resilient
17. Manage stress
18. Be creative
19. Have healthy relationships
20. Be proactive
21. Take initiative
22. Use the internet safely
23. Self-care from social media
24. Communicate well
25. Sleep and eat well

How the journal is structured

Each day focuses on a skill. You may feel strong in some of these skills already. Some might be new or difficult for you. You might feel some skills are similar and overlap. And you will definitely feel you are tapping into other skills to learn and apply new ones. As in life, nothing exists on its own. Everything is connected. It's just easier to learn new things when the information is broken down.

Each day has five sections:

- A skill
- Reflections
- Actions
- Your space
- How are you getting on?

About the ***Skill*** *section*
Alongside your academic studies, there are many other things to learn. Each day begins by discussing a skill that will help you and for you to apply to different areas of your life.

About the ***Reflections*** *section*
Building a process of reflection is important and will become a habit. This section poses questions, ideas, quotes, and facts that will trigger interesting responses from yourself. It's designed to allow you to self-reflect, and possibly make decisions about who you want to be in the world. Self-reflection is not easy. Our lives are full of distractions that can stop us thinking too deeply. Also, self-reflection can be painful, especially if we don't like the answers we uncover. However, self-reflection allows you to direct your life instead of feeling ruled by external forces.

About the ***Actions*** *section*
Taking action is where you are encouraged to practise your new skill and is key to your self-development and growth. This section provides you with some steps you can take to applying the **Learning** and **Reflections**. Treat these as small (and possibly fun!) experiments to test out your learning in a real-life context.

About the ***Your space*** *section*
You can use this space to make notes but, as getting to the heart of how we feel can be tricky, you can also use this space to express your thoughts and feelings to help you reach your truth. Use it in any way that helps you. Some ideas include:

- quoting a compliment you received that day
- jot down two or three words, make a rhyme, a couplet or a free form poem, lyrics from a song that resonate with a feeling
- draw a silly doodle or make a sketch of something
- express a positive and a negative thing
- celebrate a small or big win
- express disappointment and hope

About the ***How Are You Getting On?*** *section*
This section is for you to complete the next day or a few days later. Make self-observations about your progress in this area – what's worked and what hasn't? There is space to write this down or map your feelings. Don't worry if things are not working out. Every context is different, and it might not be easy to apply changes or see improvements quickly. Creating new habits and learning new skills takes time and effort. It's important to be kind to yourself. Do remember to note and celebrate small wins as well as the big.

Just to note, the word 'family' is meant in the broadest sense and can mean whatever family is for you.

Lastly, if you really want someone to talk to, there is a section called Need Help? at the end, listing people and services there to support you.

How to get the best out of this journal

Working through the journal daily, or a few days apart but consistently, will help you more than looking at the journal weeks apart. For example, you may decide to journal three times a week – that's fine. Consistency is key. This is because the aim is to help you integrate new behaviours to help you in life. We can only train our brain (which is a muscle), create new habits and develop new patterns of behaviour when we do things regularly. Use the reminder app on your phone, or your calendar to help you be consistent.

However, you do not need to work through the book in the order it has been set out. Work on the skills that sound interesting or most beneficial – jump back and forth or go in order. Whatever works for you is fine.

You will need about 15 minutes to complete each chapter. (Complete the **How are you getting on?** section a day or a few days later.) When you pick up the journal, choose a moment when you are unlikely to be disturbed and do not have other things to do. Turn off phones and other gadgets or put them on silent mode and facing down so you are not disturbed by notifications.

Good luck! And remember to be kind to yourself!

Your friend,

Bianca

Date:..

Day 1: RECOGNISE YOUR STRENGTHS

Strengths are the talents and abilities that are essential to who we are. They are our positive character traits that come naturally to us. We can use our strengths to help us discover our purpose and find meaningful pursuits. We can also use our strengths for managing difficult situations or completing tasks. When we use our strengths, we feel energised and in tune with who we are. Our strengths are part of what we offer to ourselves and our family, neighbourhood, school, place of work and society. When we recognise our strengths and apply them with more awareness, we build our confidence, think with more clarity, and are more likely to succeed.

Reflections

When you think about yourself, do you tend to focus more on your strengths or your weaknesses?

We all have strengths. What strengths have you gained already from your unique life experiences?

How can you use your strengths to help you achieve your goals? (Goals are discussed specifically on Day 3 but for this exercise consider those you have already set personally or in school.)

How can you use your strengths to make a unique contribution to your family or school?

Actions

- ☐ List three strengths that you have (or as many as you can identify).
- ☐ How can you use one of your strengths to help you with an area of weakness?
- ☐ How can you use these strengths to help someone in your life?
- ☐ What could you do more of to develop your strengths?

Your space

Complete this next part tomorrow or in a few days (put a reminder on your phone).

How are you getting on?

Sometimes it is easy to overlook your strengths because these come very easily to you. Remember, a lot of people don't have what you have.

(Use this space to make notes.)

Date:...

Day 2: BELIEVE IN YOURSELF

Self-belief is about having confidence in our own abilities and belief in our chances of success. It comes from feeling certain about our worthiness and the ability to achieve a goal. This includes self-esteem. If we have high self-esteem, we feel good about ourselves and our abilities. We take positive actions and approach our goals and difficult circumstances with confidence. You can trust yourself. Your ability to do well in school, college and in your personal pursuits will have a lot to do with your self-belief.

Reflections

Are you aware that you have a right to feel good about yourself?

Liking and valuing yourself provides you with the desire to do well.

Feeling like you can try something challenging is all about self-confidence.

Actions

- ☐ Name three positive things you believe to be true about yourself.
- ☐ Name one activity that you can get better at, to further build your self-confidence.
- ☐ What other new activity can you try?

Your space

Complete this next part tomorrow or in a few days.

How are you getting on?

So far so good? Great! Not doing so well? Don't worry! Just don't give up!

Remember to celebrate the small wins (this can be showing up, your effort, learning something new) to cultivate self-belief. Remember to focus your self-analysis on your *effort* and not perfection or what the end result looks like.

Date:..

Day 3: **SET YOURSELF GOALS**

A goal is an objective or target. Having goals is important. It provides us with a reason to do well at anything and helps us to focus. Your achievement in life will come from setting personal goals. Whether you want to improve your behaviour or school grades, having goals will help you to decide how to use your time, energy and resources.

Reflections

The difference between dreams and goals is that goals need to be realistic and achievable through actions you can take.

Setting yourself a goal is like setting yourself a challenge for success.

It is useful to set goals that help you grow emotionally, mentally, physically and socially.

When you have goals, it is easier to make the right choices that benefit you.

Goals can be modified. They don't have to stay the same.

Actions

- ☐ Set three goals that you can start working on.
- ☐ What steps do you need to take to achieve these goals?
- ☐ List a few actions you need to start taking to work your way up the steps. (This list might feel easier to make as you progress through the journal).
- ☐ Have fun and create a 'vision board'. A vision board reflects your goals and dreams with cut out pictures from magazines or clip art and images from the internet and attached to Google Slides (or a similar program). Keep this somewhere for you to look at.

Your space

Complete this next part tomorrow or in a few days.

How are you getting on?

Whether your goals are in the near future or far-off future, we can keep working on them now. It's important to keep going and celebrate every small effort and achievement.

Date:..

Day 4: FIND YOUR MOTIVATION

Motivation is when we are energised to get on with the tasks ahead. A key source of our motivation is to visualise our future work and life. Staying motivated can be achieved by writing down our goals (see Day 3), sticking to a schedule, and reminding ourselves of what led us to set our goal in the first place. It is useful to find a reason big enough to keep us going. For example, you might say to yourself that you want to work hard to have a thriving, fulfilling career as a writer, neurologist, sculptor, or engineer.

Reflections

When you are motivated, you do better.

We tend to be motivated to do well in the things that we enjoy.

To feel energised about the things we do not enjoy, we need to find reasons that will motivate us.

There will always be things that we dislike doing. Travellers can hate flying. Musicians can hate promotional gigs. Bankers can hate wearing suits. Being able to do things that you dislike doing is part of life and finding the motivation is key.

Actions

- ☐ Identify the things you feel motivated to do (a sport, a game, a school subject) and consider the reasons why you feel that way.
- ☐ Going back to Day 3, write down motivating reasons to achieve those goals, or you can create new ones.
- ☐ Find 1 word (or up to 3 words at the most) that will keep you motivated. It needs to make sense to you and strike a deep chord within you. It can be silly or serious. Some examples are:
    - 'Beautiful villa' (maybe you're motivated by the idea of having a villa with a beautiful pool in a tropical paradise!).
    - 'Hug' because a hug always gives you the strength to go on.
    - Some people like words like 'patience', 'calm'.
    - Perhaps something that reminds you of a previous success, like 'first place', 'gold', 'bp park run' (best performance at park run).

When your frustrations grow and your motivation dips, remember your motivation word/words to keep you going. It should bring up a feeling that helps you to stay focused. Add this word to your vision board from Day 3.

Your space

Complete this next part tomorrow or in a few days.

How are you getting on?

All good? Watch out for the days when you might lose the motivation to keep going. We all have off-days – sometimes we are just tired, or we've had a run of bad days. Keep digging in for the motivation and visualising your goals.

Date:..

Day 5: HANDLE ANXIETY

Anxiety can be described as a feeling of worry or fear that is experienced as a combination of physical sensations, thoughts and feelings. It's common to feel worried sometimes, and this is a normal part of growing up. For example, on your first day of secondary school, before an exam or maybe when you must give a presentation. Anxiety can become a problem when we feel swallowed by it. Or we can feel overwhelmed, distressed or unable to cope. If this kind of worrying goes on for a long time, it may leave you feeling exhausted and isolated. It may limit the things you are able to do.

Reflections

Symptoms of anxiety may include a racing heart, butterflies in the stomach, muscle tension, shaky hands or perhaps feel nauseous.

Sometimes we try to cope with anxiety in unhealthy ways. These include withdrawing from people, eating less or more, or even self-harming.

Actions

- ☐ Practise some mindfulness exercises aimed at managing anxiety. When you feel anxiety rising, breathe slowly and deeply and apply your practice.
- ☐ Do something that helps you feel calmer and gain perspective, like running, walking, listening to music, painting , writing or drawing.
- ☐ Find a friend you can trust and share your worries with them.

Your space

Complete this next part tomorrow or in a few days.

How are you getting on?

Sometimes, hearing the words 'don't worry' is not enough. We need help coping. If you aren't coping, or you know someone who is struggling, look at the Need Help section (near the back) to see which person or organisation can help you.

Date:..

Day 6: BE RESOURCEFUL

It's important to expect that things won't go to plan, and life is unpredictable. Being resourceful can help us in those types of situations. It's about having the ability to find quick, clever, or creative solutions to problems yourself. It means making the most of the opportunities around you and using what you already have. You may have teachers, a mentor, a relative or a friend who can give you advice. You may have access to resources, books and software to help you with your studies and special projects or career choices. Your resources includes the knowledge you have already acquired and your strengths (see Day 1).

Reflections

There are always situations, people, circumstances, and things around you that you can access and utilise for your growth and development.

Being resourceful in finding your own solutions is important and can be done even if you feel you don't know enough to go forward.

Resourcefulness can require thinking very pragmatically, flexibly or creatively.

Actions

- ☐ Who do you know that can provide you with some support or advice?
- ☐ Are there places you can you go to get some support?
- ☐ What do you have around you to support you?

Your space

Complete this next part tomorrow or in a few days. (I hope by now, you have put a reminder on your phone to get on with the journal 😊.)

How are you getting on?

Sometimes being resourceful means doing something that is not obvious, like talking to a teacher you have not spoken to before. Use what is around you: people, places and yourself.

Date:..

Day 7: MAKE SMART CHOICES

Smart choices are the ones that lead towards our goals, support our well-being and our growth. (In business, this is called a strategic choice). Not all our choices are important but we need to recognise how much we are in charge of our lives and which choices really matter. We also need to allow ourselves time to weigh up big decisions. Making a decision too rashly, and without proper consideration, can lead to regret.

Reflections

Your choices will determine your outcomes.

Always take time to think about your choices.

It's OK to change your mind and make different decisions.

Actions

- ☐ Make a list of all the choices you made today from the moment you woke up to now. (This will be a long list!) Did you choose to press the snooze button too often this morning? Did you choose to own up to something? Don't forget to include your excellent choice of opening your 25-Day journal today! 😊
- ☐ When you make your next choice, think about whether this is for your benefit.
- ☐ Check whether your choices today are consistent with your goals (from Day 3).
- ☐ What important decision can you make today that will improve your life?
- ☐ If making choices feels very confusing, you can try a tool called a SWOT Analysis. It's not fancy: it just means breaking down a choice into four components: Strengths, Weaknesses, Opportunities and Threats. Looking at a choice broken down like this can help you make an informed decision. Even if the Threat box has listed a few risks, it may feel manageable because you are aware of it. See Annex A (near the end of the book) for an example of a SWOT Analysis.

Your space

Complete this next part tomorrow or in a few days.

How are you getting on?

We can change our minds. Sometimes we need to correct our choices if they are not leading to our goals, well-being and growth.

Date:..

Day 8: PRIORITISE YOUR WELL-BEING

Our mental well-being is about how we are feeling right now, and how well we can cope with daily life. Having good well-being can help us to feel and express our emotions, have good relationships with others and enjoy the world around us. It is important for us to take care of our physical, mental, and emotional state. Pursuing hobbies, socialising and enjoying distractions is good for us. These can include watching a movie, reading a book, gaming, going for a walk, dancing, meeting up with friends or anything else we enjoy. It's important to *schedule time* to look after our well-being on a frequent basis.

Reflections

Being aware of your mind and body and what it needs means you can avoid a downward spiral where you feel overwhelmed and unable to cope.

Connecting and making time for others can support your well-being.

Hobbies and pursuits outside of school can increase your feeling of contentedness.

Physical exercise reduces stress and produces some of the brain chemicals we need to feel good.

Getting enough sleep and eating wholesome food means that you can keep problems in perspective and have enough energy for the day. Lack of sleep means that problems feel worse and eating badly can add to your problems.

Actions

- ☐ Choose a physical activity that supports your well-being today (it should take a minimum of 30 minutes). For example, yoga (there are lots of videos on YouTube), a sport, play an instrument, make a sketch.
- ☐ What new activity can you do this week to improve your well-being, e.g. visit a relative, practise some deep breathing, exercise, bake?
- ☐ Write down positive emotions that will support your well-being.
- ☐ Try a mindfulness exercise (videos are available on YouTube or there are high quality apps).

Your space

Complete this next part tomorrow or in a few days.

How are you getting on?

Our well-being can change from moment to moment, day-to-day, or month-to-month. Good well-being doesn't mean that you are always happy. Remember that happiness (and good memories) are small moments of time. Accept that sadness and low moods will happen too, but it should also be for short moments in time. If it goes on for long periods and you are finding it difficult to cope, reach out to someone you trust or see the Need Help? section at the back of the book.

Date:...

Day 9: BE KIND

We need to be kind to ourselves to be kind to others. Many of us are our own worst critics. The voices we have in our heads are often judgemental and negative. We feel an inner tussle. We defend ourselves but also agree with the criticisms. It can be exhausting and harmful to our self-esteem.

It's OK to have negative thoughts but we also need to increase the positive thoughts (see Day 13: Increase Positive Self-talk). We need to also acknowledge that thoughts are only thoughts. When we feel our worst, we tend to react to criticism worse. We get defensive. And we also treat other people badly. Contented people are usually kind, accepting of others, and generous in their thoughts and actions.

In each stage of your life, you will need to find a new acceptance of yourself, because you won't always be the same person going through the same things. At this point in your life, however, you do have a good reason to be bad at this! You can blame your brain!

The brain is always changing. During the teen-to-adult years (from ages 11-20), your brain is in rapid development (it varies from person to person), and your thought processes are changing. How you perceive the world shifts as you use different parts of your brain.

This doesn't mean you don't know the difference between right and wrong or that you can't make good decisions. Every individual is different. But if you find you keep getting into the same tricky situations, use this knowledge and your self-awareness to slow you down. Pause. Rely on sensible advice. Don't be hard on yourself. You are clearly a sensible, good-intentioned person for sticking with this journal! 😉

Reflections

Being kind to others means being kind to ourselves first. Unhappy, insecure people tend to be mean to others.

Our intentions and efforts matter more than outcomes (in many cases).

Your brain is in development and going through changes. Use your knowledge to help you.

You can also help your brain to develop well by avoiding alcohol and drugs as these delay brain development.

Mindfulness is an excellent meditative exercise which can help you to manage your thoughts and focus more. It helps to reduce stress and can make people feel more balanced and motivated.

Sleeping well and eating well helps us to manage our mood and thoughts. This will help you feel more relaxed and less tense towards yourself (and others).

Actions

- ☐ What are your negative thoughts that you notice?
- ☐ Do you acknowledge that they are just thoughts, and they aren't important? That your intention (what you want) and your effort (what you do) is what matters?
- ☐ If you have never tried mindfulness exercises, give it a go. There are lots of good apps, but there are also plenty of free explanations and practices available online. A session only lasts a few minutes. Letting go of thoughts and not attaching feelings to them requires practice – embrace the effort.

Your space

Complete this next part tomorrow or in a few days.

How are you getting on?

As with everything in this journal, it's all about practice. Things become easier with practice.

Date:...

Day 10: BE A PROBLEM-SOLVER

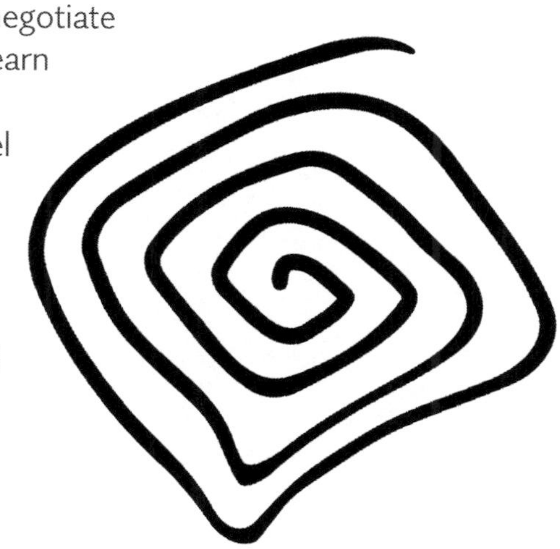

Problem-solving is an important life skill because it enables you to successfully deal with challenges and setbacks. When you're solving problems, it's good to be able to listen, think calmly, consider options, respect other people's opinions, negotiate and work towards compromises and solutions. When we learn skills and strategies for problem-solving and resolving conflicts, we not only create a way to move forward, we feel stronger and more confident. We become better able to manage our lives. For example, your friends may be arguing, but you help them reconcile. Or you may have several deadlines falling at the same time, and you deal with it by prioritising a big assignment to complete first and requesting alternative deadlines with your other teachers.

Reflections

The ability to problem-solve can stop small issues from escalating into big ones.

When you apply problem-solving skills, you are empowered to sort out conflict, be independent and overcome challenges.

Big problems become small.

Actions

- ☐ Identify and write down a current challenge, set-back or problem.
- ☐ Think about possible solutions.
- ☐ Measure the pros and cons of each solution.
- ☐ Go with the solution that offers the best results.

Your space

Complete this next part tomorrow or in a few days.

How are you getting on?

Talking about our problems can be enough – we find the answer as we speak. However, though we can try to solve our own problems, we cannot solve other people's. When it comes to the people we care about, the best thing is to be supportive and listen (and try not to problem-solve).

Date:...

Day 11: HAVE A GROWTH MINDSET

Mindset is a set of beliefs that shape how we make sense of the world and ourselves. It influences how we think, feel, and behave in any given situation. It informs how we decide to look at a situation and what conclusions we come to. Our mindset is important, because it gives direction to the course of our lives.

There are two basic mindsets: fixed and growth. If you have a fixed mindset, you believe your abilities are fixed traits and can't change. A growth mindset is about believing you can develop and improve your abilities. How we feel and what we say is often a result of our mindset. Therefore, having a growth mindset that recognises our efforts in our education, relationships, etc., means we learn and grow to be the best versions of ourselves.

Reflections

Failure or not doing well is not the end. It's about understanding that there may be another way of doing something.

We can learn from our mistakes.

We tend to be hard on ourselves. If you were to talk to yourself the way you would talk to a best friend, is there a difference? Are you more balanced or more flexible?

Actions

- ☐ Think of a task you're struggling with. How can you approach it differently?
- ☐ What negative situation have you learnt from recently?
- ☐ Think about how you give words to a negative situation. Does it sound like a fixed mindset or a growth mindset? How can you rephrase this to be more flexible and show a growth mindset?

Your space

Complete this next part tomorrow or in a few days.
How are you getting on?

Constant negative thoughts can make us feel that we cannot change or progress. It is important to recognise that we have a choice in how we view a situation. We also choose the words we give to a situation. Words have the power to change our outlooks.

Date:..

Day 12: BE CURIOUS

Trying new things gives you an opportunity to learn about yourself and can build your confidence and sense of identity. You might already have a few hobbies but trying things that you imagine you won't like is also important. Extra-curricular activities can be anything: sports, drama, Scouts and Guides, Lego-building, crafting or photography. It can be more structured like language classes, music, debating, religious instruction, swimming, or paid and unpaid jobs. It can be hard to try something new, especially if you don't know anyone else doing it. Be brave. Be open-minded. Consider taking a friend.

If cost is a problem, it may be possible to find activities that are low-cost or free. Check with your school and local community centre. Activities for young people are often subsidised by the local council. There are also some relatively low-cost pursuits such as sketching and reading (borrow books from your school or local library).

Reflections

When you try new things, you learn more about yourself and gain more confidence.

Learning new skills can open your world, helping you to see and do more and meet new people with common interests.

Having a hobby, even solitary hobbies, can increase our social skills because interesting people have interests.

Actions

- ☐ What one new thing can you try (excluding online and screen activities)?
- ☐ Find out from your school, local community and local paper about clubs and classes.
- ☐ What new hobby can you start from home?

Your space

Complete this next part tomorrow or in a few days.

How are you getting on?

It can be daunting to try new something new. Take small steps. This is for your pure enjoyment.

Date:...

Day 13: INCREASE POSITIVE SELF-TALK

We have talked about our inner thoughts and the way we talk to ourselves (see Day 9: Be Kind and Day 11: Have a Growth Mindset) and using positive words to support us more. Here, we talk about positive self-talk. It means talking to ourselves and making positive, optimistic statements that can be helpful in coping with stressful moments. We can learn to be our own personal cheerleader. Often, our words make us feel a certain way and may also lead to both negative or positive actions. Language is very powerful, so it's helpful to rephrase our words to support our well-being.

Reflections

Words are very powerful.

If you notice yourself feeling down, unmotivated, or distressed, be aware of how you are talking to yourself. Are the thoughts negative, angry, defensive, mean? Or are they reasonable, comforting, humorous, optimistic?

You have the power to challenge negative self-talk with positive self-talk.

Actions

- ☐ Name the feelings and situations that trigger negative emotions such as sadness, anger, and anxiety.
- ☐ Use these feelings as a signal to pause and become aware of yourself.
- ☐ How can you challenge negative self-talk? What positive things can you say to yourself?
- ☐ How can you reframe your words about a certain situation in your life? Examples include:
  - I'll be bad at this. / I don't have to be an expert to give it a try.
  - I made a mistake and look stupid. / Mistakes are normal.
  - I look foolish. / I've dealt with that before and I can deal with it again.
  - I will never be able to do this. / I will get through this.
  - They won't like me. / I'm fine as I am.
- ☐ Write down a positive statement to help you with when your negative talk is strong. Keep it on you so that you can remind yourself to stay strong and challenge the negative self-talk with positive self-talk.

Your space

Complete this next part tomorrow or in a few days.

How are you getting on?

Speaking positively takes time and practice. Take time to be self-aware and mindful about your thoughts and words.

Date:..

Day 14: CULTURAL AND CIVIC SKILLS

You have probably been learning in school about the importance of cultural awareness and our place, as individuals, in society. This is important as you grow and become an adult and an active citizen (even choosing not to be an active citizen is a political choice). Your appreciation and awareness of people contribute to building your positive self-image and respect for others.

Developing cultural awareness can deepen the skills we have been talking about, like reflection, kindness, positive communication and social skills. Respecting and appreciating the differences in our social background, heritage, ethnicity, race, gender and religion, creates a social consciousness that is safe and accepting.

We learn from others, and we can learn about ourselves and our differences from others too, as well as the things that are common to us all. We live in a society that we can benefit from greatly.

Reflections

Through your exposure to different people, ideas, languages, practices, foods and histories, you get the opportunity to enrich the quality of your own life and know yourself better.

When you are open-minded and accept differences but can also find common grounds, you stretch and challenge yourself.

No matter your age, you can be a positive force for peace, communication and understanding.

Culture can refer to subcultures (a culture within a culture like Goth or punk) or intellectual and artistic (like political science or ballet). Having interests and sharing those with a community can increase our own inner cultural diversity too. For example, you can be a student and belong to your school's culture. At the same time, you have your family and home culture, traditions and heritage. If you help grow vegetables in an allotment, you belong to the community there too. And if you do karate, you might enjoy the culture and of your dojo.

Actions

- ☐ Think about your attitude to difference. Do you like it or dislike it?
- ☐ Think about whether you separate the cultures you live in and, if you do, why? For example, your home culture and the way you are with your school friends.
- ☐ Try asking people about their culture. What foods do they eat? What languages do they speak?

Your space

Complete this next part tomorrow or in a few days.

How are you getting on?

People can find it hard to talk about their heritage and traditions because they aren't used to it, and when we enter mainstream institutions, like school, work or politics, we feel we should hide aspects of ourselves to be accepted by the larger social group. But when we aren't being authentic, we tend to feel less free and less happy.

Date:..

Day 15: USE HUMOUR

Humour is a great gift and a skill we can learn to use. Sometimes, there is nothing we can do about our circumstances, but we can laugh about it. We all face embarrassment and feel we won't be able to overcome it. Laughing makes it easier and reduces the sting. Sometimes we don't want to try new things because we are afraid of looking foolish. But in order to progress and succeed, we need to give permission to ourselves to look foolish – even embrace it. This is a lot less hard if we learn to laugh at ourselves. And at the end of a bad day, try to find the funny side. It really helps.

Reflections

Laughter is very healthy and having a sense of humour about yourself will make life easier.

Laughing at our circumstances can be the best therapy.

Sometimes, to get what we want, we need to be willing to look foolish and be able to laugh at ourselves.

Actions

- ☐ Are you good at laughing at yourself? Or do you feel immense upset and embarrassment? Even anger?
- ☐ Can you think back to an embarrassing situation or when you had a bad day?. Looking back, are you able to laugh about it?
- ☐ At the end of tomorrow, think back to an awkward situation. Perhaps you tripped up or a teacher scolded you. Can you see how silly it was?
- ☐ There is a balance between laughing at yourself and putting yourself down. Make sure you are not putting yourself down.

Your space

Complete this next part tomorrow or in a few days.

How are you getting on?

It can be hard to laugh when we are in the 'thick of it' but it's easier after a little time and distance. Using humour can allow us to work through our frustrations and move forwards instead of letting negative feelings linger.

Date:..

Day 16: BE RESILIENT

Resilience is the ability to withstand, adapt to, or recover from adversity and stress. Having resilience doesn't mean we avoid sadness, disappointment, or failure. But people who are resilient bounce back more easily. Resilience is also about the ability to adapt to difficult circumstances that can't be changed. Resilience also helps us to face everyday challenges like embarrassment, arguments with friends, disappointing test results, a game or sporting loss.

Reflections

Developing resilience means finding it easier to adapt to stressful situations or crises, with fewer negative effects.

'Do not judge me by my success, judge me by how many times I fell down and got back up again.'- Nelson Mandela

Actions

- ☐ Which aspect of your life do you need to become more resilient in?
- ☐ What one thing can you do to deal with a circumstance that you cannot change.
- ☐ What different way can you approach a recent failure.

Your space

Complete this next part tomorrow or in a few days.

How are you getting on?

Resilience exists in all of us. You may already have been tapping into it. If you face more serious challenges like learning difficulties and physical disabilities, family breakdown, family illness, death and grief, or bullying, your resilience is probably very strong already.

Date:..

Day 17: MANAGE STRESS

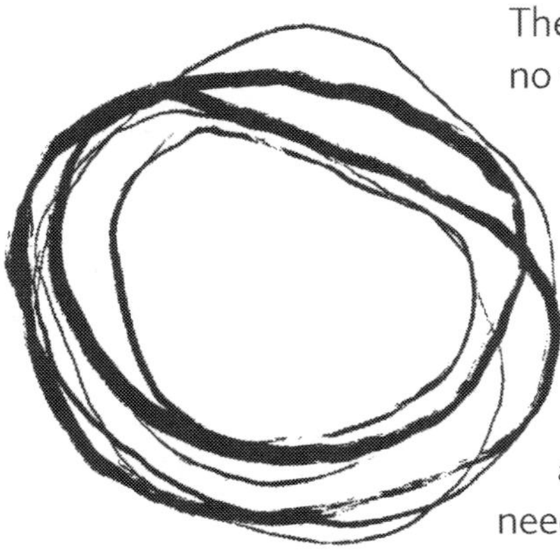

The skills discussed so far are a way of managing stress. There is no way to avoid stress completely. We all experience it, even the most solid or care-free person.

The types of stresses you face may not be things you can do much about. It could be about changes in your body, exams, fear of the future, worries about the affairs of the world, people's expectations of you, what other people think of you, gossip, crushes or relationships going wrong, etc. Small amounts of stress is OK. However, ongoing amounts of stress needs to be managed because it can be immensely harmful.

If you have gone through parts of this journal, you'll know that we can deal with stress in all sorts of ways - such as, knowing your strengths, using positive self-talk or using humour. But to help you grow further, you do need to think about stress specifically.

First, you need awareness. You need to recognise where the stress is coming from in your life or what types of situations makes you feel stressed. Second, you need to recognise when you are starting to feel stressed before it overwhelms you. Third, you need to create tactics to reduce stress.

Reflections

Stress can't be avoided but it should not overwhelm us.

Stress can impact us physically and lead to illness, disease and mental strains causing anxiety, panic attacks and depression.

Stress can be managed. We need to recognise when we feel it early and use tactics to lower our stress levels and protect our well-being.

Actions

- ☐ Identify the types of issues that cause you to feel stress.
- ☐ Identify what happens to you when you feel stressed. There are probably several feelings, behaviours and physical ailments you'll recognise, e.g. short temper, panic, sleeplessness, aches in your body, overeating, eating too little, procrastination, etc.
- ☐ Now, consider how to manage the early stages of stress. It can include:
    - Talking to someone and creating an action plan.
    - Talking to someone about things unrelated to the matter - let them know you need a laugh.
    - Physical exercise can create clarity and bring down our stress hormones.
    - Have a beverage or a snack – something soothing like a hot chocolate.

- Switch off from the stress: listen to music, dance, go for a walk, use a mindfulness app or use an online video.
- Watch a movie – avoid dystopian and sad films. Comedies and action movies are great for taking our minds off our present moods.

When your stress levels feel lower and you feel calmer, have a look at the sections of this book and see which parts might help you to manage stress better.

Your space

Complete this next part tomorrow or in a few days.

How are you getting on?

Stress affects everyone differently. Don't be afraid to talk about it.

Date:..

Day 18: BE CREATIVE

Being creative is about expressing ourselves imaginatively and uniquely or creating something to be seen, felt, heard or tasted (or a combination). It can be in response to an experience or to reflect an observation and can invoke thoughts and feelings in others. Being creative is about exploring beyond your comfort zone. Creative activities help build authentic connections with yourself and others around you.

Reflections

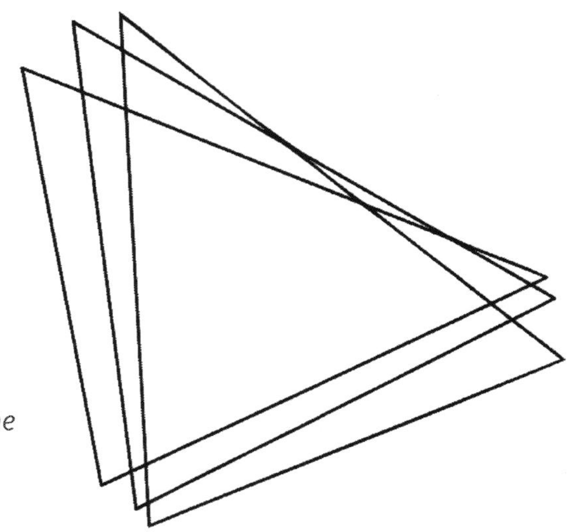

Creativity can give you a feeling of mastery.

Creativity engages your mind and can also engage your body and senses.

Creativity can help us draw out what is already within us - hidden talents and capabilities. It adds richness to our life.

We can apply creativity in everyday life, from making meals for the family, decorating a room, or apologising to someone with a drawing or a poem.

Actions

- ☐ What creative pursuits do you enjoy?
- ☐ In which areas of your life can you demonstrate creativity?
- ☐ Do you have an issue that could be resolved with some creative thinking?

Your space

Complete this next part tomorrow or in a few days.

How are you getting on?

We are all creative: making apps, Lego builds, anime drawings, knitting, canvas painting, singing, dancing, drama...it all counts. It can take courage to come out of your comfort zone and push yourself in this direction - but doing so can be immensely satisfying and liberating.

Date:..

Day 19: **HAVE HEALTHY RELATIONSHIPS**

Your family relationships and friendships may change throughout your life. Ten years ago, you wanted the company of your main carers. Ten years on, you probably seek the company of your friends. In another 10 years, you may mostly want the company of a lifelong partner or a few good friends and 10 years on from there, you might be enjoying the company of your own children or nephews and nieces, a few solid friends and family members.

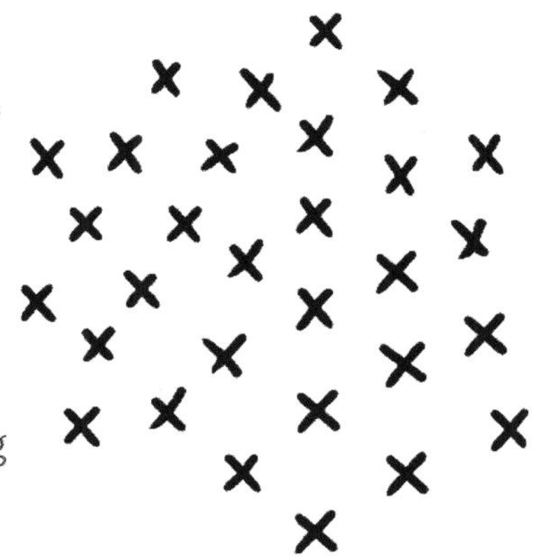

At the heart of all good relationships is respect, considerateness, acceptance and honest communication. We should expect to have conflict – it's healthy as long as each person expresses themselves reasonably, i.e. non-violently and not abusively.

Conflict can be resolved if you can be humble, listen, and put yourself in their position (empathise). You don't have to agree – but showing you understand other people is important in getting past the problem.

The ability to listen and be supportive is important. We all experience sadness, tragedy, and unfairness, illness, loss, break-ups, bereavement, divorce, family breakdown, the impact of addiction and substance abuse, gambling, debt, etc. Being supportive can help the people you care about.

It's also important to identify healthy relationships from unhealthy relationships. Good relationships are the ones you can rely on when you struggle and need a lift. Relationships which mostly cause us to feel bad about ourselves, where we are not valued or cared for and our well-being is of little importance, or we feel used and even feel threatened – these relationships and situations are the ones to walk away from. They may not always feel this way – there might be good moments that make you feel everything is OK. It can be confusing. But good relationships never make you feel unsafe, trapped, manipulated, used or violated. You should distance yourself if possible and seek advice and help where it is not possible. If there is no one in your life you can trust to help you, or you are embarrassed or feel trapped, see the Need Help? section at the end of the book.

Reflections

Healthy relationships support us.

An unhealthy relationship is one that can sometimes feel good but at other times makes us feel neglected, used, confused, manipulated, unsafe, afraid. If violence or blackmail has been used, we are definitely unsafe and should seek help.

Connection to others supports our needs to feel valued and supported.

We can support our loved ones by listening to them. You don't have to have a response or an answer. Sometimes all we need is someone to listen and care.

Actions

- ☐ Which relationships in your life do you value?
- ☐ Which relationships can you rely on?
- ☐ Do conflicts arise in your home? Are you afraid of conflict? Or do you throw yourself into conflict forcefully?
- ☐ How can you deal with conflict better? (If you are afraid, how can you be less afraid? If you are too quick to enter an argument, how can you manage yourself better?)
- ☐ What two things can you do to help create better relationships with people you want to get on better with? (E.g. offer tea or a snack, listen more, show more considerateness).

Your space

Complete this next part tomorrow or in a few days.

How are you getting on?

Relationships are not easy. Remember we get our emotional support from the relationships we keep.

Date:...

Day 20: BE PROACTIVE

Being proactive means making independent decisions, looking ahead to know where to invest your efforts now. A proactive person anticipates and seeks to avoid potential problems or obstacles. The opposite, a reactive person, waits for problems and deals with them as they occur. Proactive thinking allows you to get ahead of difficult situations and make more progress. Reactive thinking is always one step behind.

Reflections

When you are proactive, you can get things done on time or even early.

Proactivity is about looking ahead and preparing for what's to come: you can even create your own opportunities.

Being proactive allows you to take control of aspects of your life.

Actions

- ☐ Think of the times you have been reactive. How has being reactive been unhelpful to you?
- ☐ What potential obstacles can you see ahead in the following term or year ahead?
- ☐ What one thing can you do to be more proactive in your life? What will it involve? How will this benefit you?

Your space

Complete this next part tomorrow or in a few days.

How are you getting on?

It can be hard to think far ahead and long-term or to know about the consequences of our actions. Remember, it's OK to make mistakes if we learn from them.

Date:..

Day 21: TAKE INITIATIVE

Similar to being proactive, taking initiative requires the ability to see something that needs to be done and deciding to do it without someone else instructing us or asking us first. Taking initiative also means going the extra mile to make things happen. When we take initiative, we are being resourceful, proactive and possibly creative. People who show initiative tend to stand out or have an advantage.

Reflections

Deciding to do things that make things better for you or others demonstrates great thinking skills and care.

Taking initiative can open up opportunities and make things happen.

Showing initiative can take courage because you are doing something without instruction and your peers may not be doing the same.

Actions

- ☐ In what areas of your life can you take more initiative?
- ☐ Can you make a list of when taking initiative will be useful?
- ☐ Can you talk over your ideas with someone?

Your space

Complete this next part tomorrow or in a few days.

How are you getting on?

Have you found it easy? We can make mistakes even when trying to show initiative. It can also feel a bit too far out of our comfort zone. Just know it's OK to be bold sometimes.

Date:..

Day 22: USE THE INTERNET SAFELY

Internet safety skills are important for all of us. When we do not feel good about ourselves, we are more vulnerable to being taken advantage of. Being aware of your feelings means you can be more cautious of risks, such as coming into contact with people that you do not know and have never met in real life. In general, it is better to only communicate with those you know and trust and block all others. Be wary of adults posing as your age, bullies, fraudsters and aggressive marketing. All seek to harm by humiliation, theft and addiction. There are financial risks to your family too – you may end up subscribing or signing up to unfair contracts, terms or conditions or making expensive purchases.

Reflections

The internet is valuable when used wisely. It can support for your growth, development and well-being.

Not everything on the internet is for your benefit.

Much of what is on the internet is a sales pitch – very little is free. Even if you are not paying for anything, companies are harvesting your data.

There are people who make money by harming and exploiting others. People who feel low self-esteem, are lonely, worried and have problems or debt are more vulnerable.

Being a critical thinker is important when using the internet. Never give away your personal details quickly. If you feel pressured, walk away from the situation.

Actions

- ☐ What are unhelpful and helpful ways to use the internet?
- ☐ What does it mean to be a victim on the internet?
- ☐ Can you recognise times when you have felt pressured online?

Your space

Complete this next part tomorrow or in a few days.

How are you getting on?

The internet can lead to addiction, such as gambling and shopping, and can lead to unhealthy choices and slanted views of the world. Recognise your feelings (which make us vulnerable to being taken advantage of by immoral people and companies) and exert caution. Take a step back or speak to someone you know who can help you think clearly and make a safe decision.

Date:..

Day 23: SELF-CARE FROM SOCIAL MEDIA

Social media allows us to connect with friends and family and create connections and friendships across the globe with like-minded people. We can be part of wider communities based on our ideals, principles and interests. It can play a vital role in allowing us to communicate when access to information is limited. We enjoy having followers and likes – it triggers hormones that make us feel good (dopamine) and we can use social media to not just share, but to boost our self-esteem and to feel appreciated and validated as to who we are.

The reasons that make it positive are also the reasons that make it problematic. It's used as a place to bully, harass and intimidate. We share information and images that can be used against us in the future. Our information is easily harvested by big commercial companies and corrupt governments to use against us. Dopamine can be addictive and when we are not getting the dopamine, we can feel low. We can become reliant on people on social media to validate who we are because we have not built it within us, or we have lost what we had. Being constantly online and can also create a pressure of needing to always be online because we might be missing out.

We all need to know how to use social media for our benefit and be aware of the dangers. The best way to remain safe from the harms is to be aware of your dependency, create your boundaries, and manage your use conscientiously.

Reflections

How important is social media to you? Do you think you can live without using your social media apps for 72 hours? If not, why not?

Social media distorts the real world. It makes people's lives look better than it is.

It amplifies the voices of intolerant people. It can be used to manipulate us. It makes us less empathetic and tolerant.

Social media is linked to depression, social anxiety, loneliness and isolation.

Some people feel healthier by being off social media completely, or only when they want to benefit, e.g. to share a piece of news or promote something.

Creating your own rules of engagement can be empowering. You can decide what your boundaries are – what you share, like, repost and the times you log on.

Actions

- ☐ List the ways you're motivated by social media. Does it affect your behaviour, your thoughts, fears?
- ☐ Have you observed abuse? Have you been/are you being abused? What can you do?
- ☐ Create your own rules of engagement.
- ☐ Remember you have options to turn off push notifications or you can carve out non-screen times in your schedule.
- ☐ Find ways to feel good about yourself without needing validation from other people.

Your space

Complete this next part tomorrow or in a few days.

How are you getting on?

If you feel you are too reliant on social media and want it to change, consider a 'digital detox' – a temporary move away from technology and online communication for a set time. Or set a regular time that you will keep yourself physically removed from a screen and communications.

Date:...

Day 24: COMMUNICATE WELL

Communicating well is not the same as speaking or writing well. It is about expressing ourselves in healthy ways. It's also about listening to others and responding appropriately – sometimes this means not saying anything because it means you are showing understanding and not being judgemental. Good communication skills are important for all areas of our lives because it allows us to develop and grow with fewer barriers and more freedom. You will always face difficulties but learning to express your difficulties means you are far more likely to get the support you need. Communication can lead to differences of opinions and disagreement and even arguments. This is healthy and normal.

Reflections

When you are struggling, speaking up early is better than speaking up later. But speaking-up later is better than not speaking at all. No one should suffer in silence.

What you need to say is important.

When we communicate, we let others know how we feel and what we think.

When we don't communicate, we are blocking communication and not giving others a chance to understand us, and we are not truly understanding them.

Listening is also part of communication. When we listen, we are showing care and respect to others.

We don't always want to share our thoughts and feelings. Be aware of your thoughts and feelings and know when it is better to share.

Speaking our thoughts can give us clarity and we can find our answers just by saying them aloud to someone.

Actions

- ☐ Do you feel you could communicate better?
- ☐ Who do you need to listen to more?
- ☐ When you hear something that you don't like, how can you manage your negative responses better?

Your space

Complete this next part tomorrow or in a few days.

How are you getting on?

Developing good communication with people in your life can take time. Even with good intentions, if you or the person you are talking to is having a bad day, good speaking and listening can deteriorate.

Date:..

Day 25: **SLEEP AND EAT WELL**

This may not seem like a 'skill' but good sleeping and eating habits can be learnt. Learning to *understand what you need to feel your best* is really important to achieving your well-being.

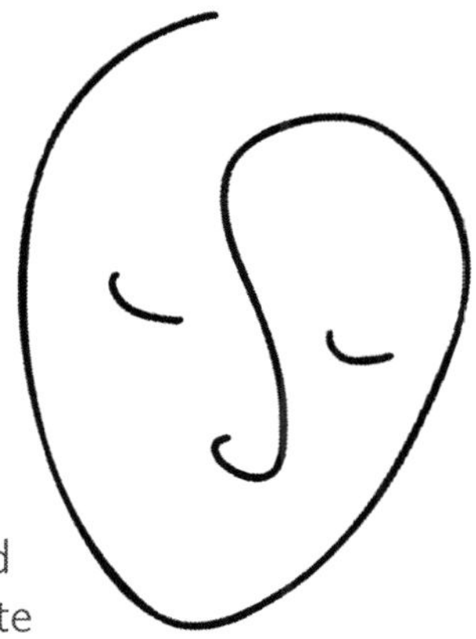

Sleep and nutrition go hand in hand. We need both to restore our body, regenerate and grow, it's good for our immune system, state of mind, brain chemistry, hormonal balance, for energy, the ability to think and react ... The research is ever-growing when it comes to the benefits of sleeping and eating well.

There are so many things that impact sleep – usually related to stress, worry and distractions. Stress, poor sleep and not being organised also cause us to eat badly. Our hunger hormones increase (ghrelin), and our feeling-full hormones decrease (leptin). It can also cause us to look for food with higher levels of sugars and fats because our body wants to compensate for the lack of energy with more food.

Besides all this, your age group is in a state of change. You need more sleep and you need more (healthy) food.

The temptation to be online, binge-watch late at night or eat junk food will always be there. Finding the strength to change bad habits comes from self-love. When we love and respect someone or something, we often stand up for them and we don't harm them.

Reflections

Our bodies need sleep and good nutrition. Negative thoughts magnify our problems and we are less capable of problem-solving. There is evidence that 'sleeping on it' and 'things looking better in the morning' is true.

Lack of sleep increases stress and our perception of problems. Stress can increase lack of sleep. It's a vicious cycle.

Lack of sleep can cause us to eat badly. This affects our health and our well-being.

Eating high-fat foods and high-sugar foods is fine occasionally. Freshly prepared, home-cooked meals is always much better.

Bad eating habits can affect sleep, such as having caffeinated or sugary beverages.

Self-love is important. When we care about ourselves, we take care of our needs. You deserve to sleep, and you deserve good, nourishing food.

Actions

- ☐ Your body is a magnificent thing, capable of so much. Do you believe your body deserves to be taken care of?
- ☐ If you don't know how to improve your sleep, there's a lot on the internet about how to sleep well. Find what works for you.
- ☐ There is a lot of information about eating well (it is better to refer to government health websites instead of influencers and brands). In what ways can you improve your nutrition? Can you cook a meal once a week or learn from someone? Can you eat more fruit and vegetables and limit the junk?
- ☐ It can help to involve our families when it comes to nutrition. Try talking to your family about making some simple changes to make family meals and grocery shopping healthier.

Your space

Complete this next part tomorrow or in a few days.

How are you getting on?

Do you feel a difference?

Every time you choose to sleep or eat better, it means your body benefits. Aim for small gradual changes. Try doing a mindfulness exercise before going to bed and see if that helps you to drop off a little quicker.

The End

You've reached the end!

A BIG WELL DONE!!!

Well … it's not quite the end. There will always be more to learn about yourself and new skills to apply as you go through life. But you have the grounding to take on challenges, achieve, and manage your well-being! Even if you skipped some pages or feel some skills are not easy to implement yet, that's OK – JUST CELEBRATE!

Please keep this book. Come back to it when you need it. Keep it as a memento – a reminder to yourself that you can make things happen with some effort. Flick through the book and find your notes - your wins, your lows, your perseverance. In your adult life, when you suddenly come across this journal, I have no doubt that you will be impressed with yourself. I know that I am impressed and very proud of you.

If you want to send me feedback, I would love to hear from you. Please get in touch at **bianca@parentpower-ed.co.uk**.

All the very best,

Your proud friend,

Bianca

Need Help?

If you are worried and need help, there are many people and charities you can go to. Many adults are there to help you, even if they don't personally know you.

The best person to choose will depend on you, your particular situation and the adults in your life.

In an ideal world, parents or carers would be the first and best people to talk to. But it's not an ideal world. You may have good reasons to feel that you cannot turn to your parent or carer.

Never think there is no one for you.

The following people have a duty to support you and get you the right help.

- A teacher who you like
- Your Head of Year
- Your GP
- A youth worker or social worker (if you have one presently)

Below is a list of organisations you can contact directly.

Childline

Phone no: 0800 1111
Website: childline.org.uk
Childline support children and young people in the UK. There is a free helpline and 1-2-1 online chats with counsellors.

FRANK

Phone no: 0300 123 6600
Website: talktofrank.com
FRANK offers confidential advice and information about drugs, their effects and the law.

SAFELINE

Phone no: 0808 800 5007 (young people's helpline)
Website: safeline.org.uk
Safeline has helplines for young people and adults who have experienced sexual abuse and rape

Anxiety UK

Phone no: 03444 775 774
Text: 07537 416 905
Website: anxietyuk.org.uk/get-help/
Anxiety UK is a user-led organisation that supports anyone with anxiety, phobias, panic attacks or other anxiety-related disorders.

Annex A: AN EXAMPLE OF A SWOT ANALYSIS

Referring to Day 7 (Make Smart Choices), you can use a SWOT Analysis chart to help you decide if a choice is right for you or not. See an example below (SWOT stands for Strengths, Weaknesses, Opportunities and Threats).

Question: Should I take driving lessons now or later?

Strengths	Weaknesses
I feel ready I already have money for 5 lessons I can ask my friend's driving instructor (who is good apparently, but she sounds a bit odd) I have just done the theory and it will expire in 24 months I have a job starting in the summer and I'll have enough money...	I *only* have money for 5 lessons I don't have money for more lessons or the test (yet) I might need a lot of lessons because I might not be good I don't know anyone who I can practise with in between lessons (mum just sold her car) If I pass, I haven't got money for a car If I buy a car, I haven't got money for insurance.
Opportunities	**Threats**
Birthday is approaching and I'll get more money I begin my job in the summer and will have money (but I also want other things) Summer holidays are approaching, so I have the time for lessons Maybe mum will buy a car again and get insurance if I offer to share some of the costs...? I could get an extra job (tutor a year 6 kid?) to help with money ...	I might not get much birthday money I might not like the driving instructor (who really sounds a bit odd, but is good apparently) An extra job would reduce my time for fun and might even reduce my availability to take lessons!

How you choose to analyse a SWOT chart is up to you but seeing information laid out this way can be very helpful. We tend to analyse information using data, reasoning and emotion/instinct/bias. So your view of the chart might be different to someone else. The threats may seem insurmountable. The weaknesses may seem too many. Or the strengths may look as though they can support the weaknesses and threats. The opportunities may seem too good to resist. It may seem that the strengths and opportunities together outweigh the weaknesses and threats. The decision you make will feel right because you have considered different aspects.

There are many other types of tools to help people make decisions, so if this doesn't work for you, have a search online for 'decision-making tools'.

Printed in Poland
by Amazon Fulfillment
Poland Sp. z o.o., Wrocław

19894669R00054